first published in 2022
in partnership with
prototype publishing
71 oriel road
london e9 5sg
uk

*Little Dead Rabbit* was printed on the
presses of SIA Jelgavas Tipogrāfija in
Latvia. Typeset in Lelo Medium
(Camelot Typefaces) and printed on
Munken Pure.

With thanks to editor Matthew Caley,
Arts Council England,
print-tech-wizard Alexey Murashko,
our respective partners Philip Hancock
and Yashu and of course, thank you
Jess Chandler, publisher *extraordinaire*.

A CIP record for this book is available
from the British Library
ISBN: 978-1-913513-28-3

www.prototypepublishing.co.uk
@prototypepubs

( )   (         )      p      prototype

# Little Dead Rabbit

That          line     is     a       dot

that    went    for     a       walk

it              walk            &               walk            {walk

walk            walk            walk            walk

walk            walk}

walk            &                walk

it              drag

its             feet

like            road        marks


d     i     v     v      y      i      n      g


up           the         street

This            is            my            travelbeat

heartbeats

rain        feet

Look,        a              rabbit


dead        in      the     cold    on      its     ownsome


peaceful      &       traumatic


like      a       dozing child


its      scut    limp    by      its     belly

a          comma

breaks        the       line       with

a         tear

beat




,

no          ifs          &          buts          or

LOOK!          No          hands

no          ifs          &          buts          or

Look!          No          hands

All    death is    under    suspicious    circumstance

little        rabbit

hang            its        head

little        line        of        mine        ,

chain-chewing        mutt        must  have  got

it

shift

WO O O O        F        F

Hm-hm.           All                         right.

Rubbed           its           bleary            eyes

little         rabbit,       a       whole        other   world

ran     rings        around              its     dangly

neck

Night  is      the      sun         gone            cold.

Like       the       voice of       a       loved       one       who       has

died

that    speaks to       us       in       inaudible       consonants

like       a       freight       train rumbling       in       its

tracks

&       little                              rabbit

running                                            alongside

manoeuvres

in              goodbye                        whimpering

D R E A M O N

stretched itself to a scream —

long overshoots

a small efficient everything

always is not from here

a      question      mark examining      its      periphery

its      doppelgänger,      shadowboxer,

hero,      lover

torturer,      butcherer,      Other

pat        pat        little                    rabbit

The    line    pats    itself    down.    I    pat    myself    down.

I'm              fine.    It's                    fine.

Sleep        sleepy        little        dead        rabbit

         Night            has    grown            arms

   spill        past        dumb        parakeets

      &        unoccupied        park        benches

         their    bioluminescent    tendrils    bloom

B        L        O        O        M

little    paws    clenched    in    prayer   no   longer   cold.

Streetlights    suffer in   the   darks.

The  line  speeds up  as  if in  a  nature  film

sped  up  clouds  float  like  eggs

&    drown

you  stand in  for  why

I draw figures with my finger through the sky

like      Asta Nielsen   in   the   silent      movies

to      mark sadness      when      summer      dies

&      voices sshhhhhhhhed      their      light

I draw   figures   with   my   finger through   the   sky

&   voices   sshhhhhhhhed   their   light

*hors de combat*


lapis lazuli


lionfish


shimmering                                    carp


insect   noises


little      little    rabbit     in     the    moon

all     drained     of     shape     &     colour

all     all   all     in     time's overflow

*nolens*     *volens*   a   line

not     mine     NOT     MINE

fear          never          stops          walking


but

fear          never          stops

walking          fear     is     a     faithful

shadow

hoppa

hophop                              hophop

jumpon          over

I     said     no     ifs     &     buts     or     hands

LOOK!          no          hands

Headlights          big     as     the     cross-eyed          moon loop        little        rabbit

through        the        air        like        a        finger        putting

you        there

little        rabbit

Headlights        big        as        the        cross-eyed        moon

0

O

FLY FLY & L

P

Land    on    the    grass    little    rabbit

drops    of    blood    bleeding    in    the    grass

Arh          &          Weh!


stiff          &          panting –

          *quelle*                    *surprise*


          roundandround


must          we          go          why


          and


          why&why

turns     the     corner   through    the    prehistory

of      you    &     me

one    part    is    lonely    &    happiness    too

softly

soft

so          softly

--- can          you          hear? ---

the              final        panting

heh-heh-heh-heh

heart-jolts

hush

now      little      rabbit

who     among     the     angels     would     have     heard

it          cry          out

above          the          traffic

little          dead          rabbit

drift          now

to     the     periphery     of     all     space

&            shapes

stars     &     patterns

piercing     the     billowing     night

so slowly ------- -  -  -  - - slower -  -  - -

sway          & -  -  - -

cities

glow          forgiving          from          afar

little                    rabbit

HOP          HOP          HOP          on over

it's     only     a     line     little     rabbit

with     a     start     &     a     jolt

in     a     few     more     shadows     gone

a     dot     that     went     for     a     walk.

If you are holding a copy of *Little Dead Rabbit*, chances are you are holding a 170 x 225mm, 64-page book that made it across the border as contraband. At the time of *Little Dead Rabbit* going to press (August 2021), the border between the UK and the EU has become impervious, obstructing the movement of books, including poetry books printed in Latvia: "since Brexit, deliveries have become very difficult and expensive due to new and as yet unclear customs procedures."

We had no choice but to take care of shipment ourselves.
After all, borders need to be porous for art, poetry, music and ideas to thrive.

Without wishing to share too many details of our poetry-book-smuggling-operation, other than that it will involve trains, a car, a ferry, a blanket, a bottle of vodka, a Channel crossing and plenty of finger-crossing, wish us bon voyage! May poetry live high! May poetry live long!

Astrid and Zigmunds

During the lockdown of 2020/21 poet Astrid Alben and graphic designer Zigmunds Lapsa worked closely together on *Little Dead Rabbit*, a book-length poem that is part adult fairy-tale, part concrete poem about a little dead rabbit the poet found on the verge of a road.

Ostensibly a poem about death, the small corpse is equally a meditation on healing and joy.

Lapsa is known for his handmade designs and for this book he made a series of inventive, abstract die-cuts that weave into and around the gasps and gaps of language. This creates an inescapable interplay between text and image, changing and challenging the direction of reading at every page-turn.

Alben's poems are inventive, bizarre and dynamic, and go looking for the elastic extremities of language. She was born in the Netherlands but moved to England at a young age. Forever attempting to get a grip on the bilingual brain, Alben wrote *Little Dead Rabbit* at the same time as the Dutch version, *Klein dood konijn*. Other works include *Ai! Ai! Pianissimo* (2011) and *Plainspeak* (2019). *Little Dead Rabbit* is meant for poetry lovers (including young readers) and anyone fascinated by the interplay between text and image.